ORPHEUS AND EURYDICE

Jeremy Dobrish

I0139715

BROADWAY PLAY PUBLISHING INC
224 E 62nd St, NY NY 10065-8201
212 772-8358
BroadwayPlayPub.com

ORPHEUS AND EURYDICE
© 2001 by Jeremy Dobrish

Cover photo: Michael Gottlieb

First published by B P P I in June 2001
This edition: June 2017
978-0-88145-722-3

Book design: Marie Donovan
Original copy editing: Sue Gilad
Page make-up: Adobe Indesign
Typeface: Palatino

ORPHEUS AND EURYDICE was first produced by adobe theatre company, opening on 11 October 2000. The cast and creative contributors were:

ARISTAEUS	Arthur Aulisi
HERCULES/SISYPHUS	Jeremy Brisiel
HOMELESSIUS/#2/TEIRESIAS	Vin Knight
EURYDICE	Kathryn Langwell
ORPHEUS	Andrew Elvis Miller
DEATH/ATALANTA	Erin Quinn Purcell
TANTALUS/JASON	Adam Smith
ANDREA/BACCHE/#1	Jennifer Ward
Director	Jeremy Dobrish
Set design	Matthew E Maraffi
Lighting design	Michael Gottlieb
Costume design	Meganne George
Original music	Lewis Flinn
Sound design	Chris Todd
Choreography	Erin Quinn Purcell
Video design	J Mole
Photography	Jeff George Photographic
Assistant director	Tamara Fisch
Dramaturgs	Jordan Schildcrout, Lisa Timmell
Guitarist	Cameron Greider

CHARACTERS

ANDREA, *a V J for N T V*

HERCULES, *he's as strong as he sounds. An Argonaut.*
ORPHEUS' *drummer*

JASON, *as in "Jason and the Argonauts".* ORPHEUS' *bass player. He speaks with a rock star's British accent.*

ORPHEUS, *the greatest musician in history. An Argonaut*

#1, *an assistant of* DEATH

BACCHE, *a bacchante nymph. Perhaps from the Valley*

ARISTAEUS, ORPHEUS' *manager*

EURYDICE, *a wood nymph*

ATALANTA, *the fastest mortal alive*

SISYPHUS, *condemned to spend eternity in the Underworld perpetually pushing a boulder up a hill*

TANTALUS, *condemned to spend eternity in the Underworld thirsty, surrounded by water but unable to drink*

HOMELESSIUS, *condemned to spend eternity in the Underworld just shy of change for food*

TEIRESIAS, *a blind old oracle*

DEATH, *a beautiful and somewhat freakish woman. Cool. In control. Deadly*

#2, *an assistant of* DEATH. *A fan of* ORPHEUS

To reduce the cast size you could double and triple. For example: ORPHEUS, ARISTAEUS, HOMELESSIUS/#2/ TEIRESIAS, HERCULES/SISYPHUS, TANTALUS/JASON, EURYDICE/DEATH/ATALANTA, AND ANDREA/ BACCHE/#1, *bringing the cast requirements to 5 men and 2 women.*

PRODUCTION NOTES

The play is divided into four sections, each marked by a projection. Each section should have a very different feel—

"Life Before Eurydice" is a prologue of sorts. It should be fast and dreamlike. ORPHEUS should never leave the stage; rather, characters and sets should change and swirl around him.

"Orpheus and Eurydice" is the main body of the play and should feel the most conventional with the exception of scene 18/19, which should have more in common with the next section and should serve to transition us that way.

"Orpheus in the Underworld" is the most poetic and should be the most striking in terms of production concept.

"Life after Eurydice" is an epilogue of sorts and should return to the swirling, dreamlike motions of the Prologue.

This play was written over the course of six years and was aided by the thoughtful advice of many people too numerous to mention. I am especially grateful to the cast and designers who added immeasurably to the play during both its development and rehearsal process.

"Descend, so that you may ascend"
Augustine

PROLOGUE

(As the audience enters, the whole theatre should feel like it is a concert. Orpheus and "In Your Thrace" T-shirts are being sold. Beer, etc)

(The lights go out and we hear a very large group of people chanting, "Orpheus/Orpheus" etc. We hear the voice of ANDREA, *a woman in her twenties.)*

ANDREA: *(V O)* How's everyone doing tonight?

(The crowd roars.)

ANDREA: *(V O)* I'm Andrea Siffolopolous from N T V news and…oh man, I can barely say the words. Ladies and gentlemen…"In Your Thrace".

(The crowd goes nuts as if the band has taken the stage. We hear drumsticks being clacked together and a voice say:)

VOICE: *(V O)* 1-2-3-4.

(Instant silence and a pinspot on ORPHEUS' *disembodied head. We hear the wind.)*

(The sound of a huge flash. A flurry of activity as characters come in and out, overlapping both to ORPHEUS *and the audience as appropriate, speaking lines from later in the play as the next scene gets set.)*

ARISTAEUS: They tore his head off.

BACCHE: If you could just, like, give me a tape or whatever that would be like, totally the bomb.

ARISTAEUS: For all the things you can see, you sure are blind.

TANTALUS: Funny to actually find someone looking for death instead of running away.

TEIRESIAS: Stare into a mirror long enough and you'll see death creep up and overtake you.

ARISTAEUS: She said, "Don't tell him the truth."

HERCULES: Hey what's that smell? It smells like death.

ARISTAEUS: You are washed out to sea, floating on a wave of faceless fans.

TEIRESIAS: You cannot escape your destiny.

TANTALUS: You cursed Gods of the underworld.

HERCULES: Yesterday's faith is today's fable.

ATALANTA: She said that her name would become synonymous with love.

BACCHE: You sure you don't want to like try again?

(Projection: Life before Eurydice)

ACT ONE

Scene One
A HOTEL ROOM

(The lights come up on a bed. There is an empty alcohol bottle nearby. BACCHE *and* ORPHEUS *sit up in the bed basically undressed.)*

(They dress as needed over the course of the scene.)

BACCHE: You sure you don't want to like try again?

ORPHEUS: I'm sorry.

BACCHE: Is this, like, the first time you…?

ORPHEUS: No.

BACCHE: Really?

ORPHEUS: Mmm.

BACCHE: Why? Do you think?

ORPHEUS: The pills. The booze. It's gotta be.

BACCHE: Because, I mean, like you're like a famous rock star and stuff. You can have, like, anyone you want.

ORPHEUS: Yeah. I know. I do.

BACCHE: So like, I gotta ask…why me? Why'd you pick me?

ORPHEUS: I didn't. My manager did.

BACCHE: But like why do you think he picked, like, me out of that crowd of Bacchantes for you?

ORPHEUS: I don't know.

BACCHE: (*Trying to get* ORPHEUS *interested again*) You didn't make any special requests? You didn't say like: (*Substitute any particular features of the actress playing* BACCHE*)* get me a woman with like, long blonde hair, or big like breasts, or long like legs, or…?

ORPHEUS: I said get me a woman who doesn't talk much.

BACCHE: Oh. Like. Sorry.

ORPHEUS: Look, I'm really tired.

BACCHE: The concert was totally amazing.

ORPHEUS: Thanks.

BACCHE: The bomb. I can't believe the tour is over. The first tour of Orpheus and In Your Thrace and I am like here to experience and like celebrate the end of it.

ORPHEUS: Would you mind? I just want to get some sleep.

BACCHE: Oh. You want me to, like, go and stuff?

ORPHEUS: Please.

BACCHE: O K. (*She starts getting dressed.*) Cause you know we could just like try it again.

ORPHEUS: That's O K. Thanks anyway.

BACCHE: I understand. O K, look, I'll like go and stuff, but just tell me one thing.

ORPHEUS: What?

BACCHE: How do you…like…do it?

ORPHEUS: Do what?

BACCHE: Write songs like that?

ORPHEUS: Like what?

BACCHE: To write songs that change the course of like rivers, tame wild like animals, cause the like trees to...

ORPHEUS: When I need to sing something like when I was an Argonaut for example, on the boat, it just comes out, from my...

BACCHE: But that was, like, different, right? I mean, now you're like a commercial success. How did you get from like there to like here?

ORPHEUS: I don't know. I guess I made a deal.

BACCHE: *(Coming onto him)* A deal?

ORPHEUS: Yeah.

BACCHE: I'll make a deal.

ORPHEUS: Yeah?

BACCHE: What's behind curtain number one?

(BACCHE *kneels on the floor, completely covered by a blanket, giving* ORPHEUS *a blowjob as he sits on the edge of the bed.)*

(The lights change. ARISTAEUS *enters.)*

ARISTAEUS: That was unbelievable.

ORPHEUS: I know.

ARISTAEUS: That music? How did you do it?

ORPHEUS: I don't know.

ARISTAEUS: You outplayed the Sirens.

ORPHEUS: I know.

ARISTAEUS: You saved the boat. We never could have... the Argonauts could not have succeeded without you.

ORPHEUS: It was unbelievable.

ARISTAEUS: Orpheus, this is a gift.

ORPHEUS: It is.

ARISTAEUS: You have to share this gift. With people? A band. We've got to. Somehow. I don't know. Hercules, Jason, you, a band.

ORPHEUS: You could be in it.

ARISTAEUS: Me?

ORPHEUS: Sure, why not?

ARISTAEUS: I don't play an instrument.

ORPHEUS: You could play the tambourine or something. You could be our manager.

ARISTAEUS: Aristaeus Records.

ORPHEUS: Too long.

ARISTAEUS: Arista Records.

ORPHEUS: Perfect.

ARISTAEUS: I would do anything to be a part of this. You make a record, go on tour.

ORPHEUS: I don't know though.

ARISTAEUS: Why not?

ORPHEUS: I don't know if I could do it.

ARISTAEUS: Of course you can do it.

ORPHEUS: I don't know if it would work.

ARISTAEUS: Why not?

ORPHEUS: Well on the boat I just put my faith in the music and played.

ARISTAEUS: So?

ORPHEUS: I don't know. It would be different if I had to sing, if I had to write…

ARISTAEUS: Big O, you have a gift. You need to share that gift. There are millions of people out there who want, who need, to hear your music.

ORPHEUS: I could change their lives.

ARISTAEUS: You could.

ORPHEUS: I'm just…

ARISTAEUS: Scared. I know. So what? It's certainly no scarier than outplaying the Sirens.

ORPHEUS: It would be kind of cool to be a rock star.

ARISTAEUS: Way cool.

ORPHEUS: Chicks in hotels.

ARISTAEUS: Chicks in hotels.

ORPHEUS: O K, I'll do it.

ARISTAEUS: You'll do it?

ORPHEUS: We'll do it together.

(ARISTAEUS *pulls the blanket away.* BACCHE *has vanished.*)

(*The lights change.* HERCULES *and* JASON *enter with champagne glasses for all.*)

JASON: I'd like to make a toast: when we returned with the Golden Fleece we were Argonauts, Jason and the Argonauts. And you guys know, Orpheus, Aristaeus, Hercules, I am and always shall be eternally grateful for all of your help. Now we are In Your Thrace, Orpheus and In Your Thrace. And I just want you guys to know how proud I am to be a part of this band. And to do what I can. To contribute. I love playing the bass. And I look forward to more albums, more tours, and more time with you guys. My best friends in the world.

(*They clink and drink.*)

ARISTAEUS: O K, my turn. Orpheus: your music. Man, I mean, just wow. Who could have known that the album would have sold so well? The tour? When you and I first talked about this, you remember? I had no idea how big this could get. You're a fucking genius and I look forward to managing your rock star ass into eternity.

(They clink and drink. They look at HERCULES.*)*

HERCULES: Me? O K. When we first went out on this tour I had no idea how fulfilling it would be in terms of how very much I am getting laid.

(They clink and drink.They look at ORPHEUS.*)*

ORPHEUS: Um. I just think it's incredible what you guys have done for me. I never dreamed my life could have been this exciting, this fulfilling and this…I don't know, meaningful. You had faith in me and for that I am eternally grateful.

(They clink and drink.)

ORPHEUS: I'm gonna take some time, write some, try to write some songs, and then it's back to the studio for a second album.

ARISTAEUS, HERCULES, JASON: Here here.

(All glasses together like the Four Musketeers)

Scene Two
IN THE WOODS

(The hotel bed is replaced by a rock as JASON, HERCULES, *and* ARISTAEUS *exit.* ORPHEUS *sits on the rock and plugs an electric guitar into it. He plays a few chords like the beginning of a song [Think the opening of "Smells Like Teen Spirit"]. Stops, tries again, finally launches into it. He stops suddenly and looks up as if he heard something. Throughout the scene he addresses an unseen person. In parentheses [solely for the actor's benefit] is what* ORPHEUS *hears.)*

(Would you mind keeping it down?)

ORPHEUS: What? Oh. Sorry. I didn't know anyone could hear.

(Pause) (I'm trying to sleep)

ORPHEUS: I really just thought I was alone. It is the middle of nowhere.

(Pause) (That's why it's a good place to sleep)

ORPHEUS: Yes, I guess that would make it a good place to sleep.

(Pause) (What was that that you were playing?)

ORPHEUS: Oh that? It was nothing. A song.

(Pause) (A song?)

ORPHEUS: Just a song I was…writing. Trying to write.

(Pause) (It's very loud.)

ORPHEUS: Yes, I guess it is very loud. That seems to be the thing these days.

(Pause) (Too bad.)

ORPHEUS: Soft and then loud actually. Like the Pixies.

(Pause) (Don't you mean the Sirens?)

ORPHEUS: No. Not the Sirens, The Pixies.

(Pause) (The Pixies?)

ORPHEUS: The band the Pixies. Not the actual…Pixies.

(Pause) (I've never heard of them.)

ORPHEUS: You've never heard of the Pixies? What, do you live out here in the woods and have no contact with civilization?

(Pause) (Pretty much.)

ORPHEUS: Really? But you've heard of the Sirens of course.

(Pause) (Of course.)

ORPHEUS: What they say is true you know: that the sweetness of the Siren's song is so enchanting that men will forget everything they're doing and die of hunger.

(Pause) (How do you know?)

ORPHEUS: I know because I've heard them.

(Pause) (You have?)

ORPHEUS: Mm-hmm.

(Pause) (But you didn't die of hunger.)

ORPHEUS: No. No I didn't die of hunger. You have a pretty voice. Quiet but pretty. What's your name?

(Pause) (Eurydice.)

ORPHEUS: Eurydice. That's a beautiful name. Why don't you come out here so I can see you?

(Pause) (I really just want to get some sleep.)

ORPHEUS: O K, I'm sorry I disturbed you. I suppose I should leave you to your... sleeping.

Scene Three
REHEARSAL STUDIO

(On another part of the stage JASON *and* HERCULES *enter and set up their instruments and microphones.)*

ORPHEUS: I met a girl.

HERCULES: That's a shock.

JASON: You did? That's great.

ORPHEUS: Well, not really met, I haven't really met her, I've talked to her.

JASON: What's her name?

ORPHEUS: Eurydice. She's a wood nymph.

HERCULES: Oh. Now. You gotta watch those wood nymphs.

JASON: Hercules.

HERCULES: No seriously. Sexy as hell, but flighty like the wind.

ORPHEUS: She's…there's something about her. I don't know. Just…

HERCULES: Turn their back on you in an instant.

ORPHEUS: She made me feel nervous and calm at the same time. Like even though I couldn't see her, she could see me, through me.

HERCULES: But sexy as hell, did I mention that?

JASON: Well, you have to meet her I guess, ask her out or something.

ORPHEUS: I'm gonna marry her. You wait and see. I can just feel it.

JASON: I can't wait to meet her.

ORPHEUS: Yeah. Me too.

HERCULES: Now, be careful with the marriage thing.

ORPHEUS: What?

HERCULES: You just don't want to rush into anything. Most married people I know? Not happy.

ORPHEUS: You and Daenaria are happy.

HERCULES: She's my second wife. Remember Megara?

JASON: Whatever happened to her?

HERCULES: I killed her.

JASON: Right. I knew it was something like that.

ORPHEUS: But Daenaria?

HERCULES: All I'm saying is I'm a big man. I got big appetites, let's just leave it at that.

ORPHEUS: (To JASON) What about you and Medea?

JASON: He's got you there Hercules. I am completely in love with Medea. She's an amazing woman. And a wonderful mother.

HERCULES: Just be careful. That's all I'm saying. No need to rush into anything.

JASON: So we gonna hear this new song or what?

ORPHEUS: Oh yeah. Of course. O K. It goes like this. *(He picks up a guitar. He strums a few chords. It's not very good and he knows it.)* It's just a start. What do you think?

JASON: I think we're gonna make a fortune.

HERCULES: I think we're gonna get laid like little fuckin' bunnies.

Scene Four
IN THE WOODS

(JASON and HERCULES exit with their instruments as ORPHEUS goes back to the rock. He sits on the rock and plugs his electric guitar into it. He starts to play the opening chords of his song. Stops. Looks around. Nothing. Does it again. The same. One more time. Then he stops suddenly and looks up as if he heard something. This time we hear a faint whisper representing EURYDICE's voice though we can never make out the words.)

(Would you mind keeping that down?)

ORPHEUS: Oh. Sorry.

(Pause) (Oh, it's you again. Did you come out here to intentionally disturb my sleep?)

ORPHEUS: No, of course I didn't mean to…I'm sorry. I just had a question for you.

(Pause) (Yes?)

ORPHEUS: Well… that song I was playing, do you like it?

(Pause) (I don't think I do. Nope.)

ORPHEUS: Why not?

(Pause) (I don't know. It doesn't really seem like the kind of song that could compete with the Sirens.)

ORPHEUS: No, it doesn't seem like the kind of song that could compete with the Sirens. That's exactly what I wanted to talk to you about.

(Pause) (What about it?)

ORPHEUS: Well it's not even really a song, it's just me banging away, but everyone seems to like it anyway. Trying to write doesn't work, it's only when I play from my...

(Pause) (Soul?)

ORPHEUS: Yes. Soul.

(Pause) (Well, I'm no musician...)

ORPHEUS: No, I know you're not a musician, but I just thought...

(Pause) (Look I really do need to get some sleep...)

ORPHEUS: Sleep? You sure do sleep a lot. Wait. Don't go. Please. I...Can I just see you?

(Pause. She steps out though unseen to us [as if she is standing in a wing or behind the audience or something]. He sees her. She takes his breath away.)

ORPHEUS: Oh my. You're very beautiful Eurydice. Have you ever heard of a singer called Orpheus, Eurydice?

(Pause) (Orpheus? No.)

ORPHEUS: No? Oh well, whatever. Never mind.

(Pause) (What about him?)

ORPHEUS: Well it's just...his music tames beasts, changes the course of rivers, and is even more enchanting than the song of the Sirens. At least it used to be. That's how the Argonauts got past them. He played. You've heard of the Argonauts.

(Pause) (Look, I'm just a wood nymph…)

ORPHEUS: Well…even a wood nymph might have heard of…Look, I just thought…

(Pause) (You just thought what?)

ORPHEUS: I just thought you might like to get a burger with me.

Scene Four A
REHEARSAL STUDIO

(On another part of the stage JASON *and* HERCULES *enter and set up their instruments and microphones.)*

ORPHEUS: She said yes.

JASON: To a date?

HERCULES: Who?

JASON: That's great.

ORPHEUS: I feel like I'm walking on air.

JASON: Congratulations.

HERCULES: Who, who, who?

ORPHEUS: As soon as she said yes I started singing. It just came out. I haven't felt like that since…

JASON: Since when?

ORPHEUS: Since the boat.

HERCULES: Well, let's hear it.

ORPHEUS: The new song?

HERCULES: Yeah.

ORPHEUS: Yeah? O K, well it was like this.

(Pinspot on ORPHEUS. *The sound of wind. Lights restore.* HERCULES *and* JASON *look disgusted.)*

ORPHEUS: It was better before, when I sang it to her, but I mean, what do you think?

JASON: Orpheus?

ORPHEUS: Yeah?

HERCULES: Seriously?

(Projection: Orpheus and Eurydice)

Scene Five
A BAR

(ARISTAEUS and ATALANTA sit at a bar table drinking.)

ATALANTA: We're talking about the same Eurydice?

ARISTAEUS: Eurydice. Eurydice... It would be so much easier if people had last names. Eurydice. Orpheus' girlfriend Eurydice.

ATALANTA: Well she's more than that to him.

ARISTAEUS: She is, isn't she?

ATALANTA: They met, what...?

ARISTAEUS: Like two months ago or something. I was starting to think she doesn't exist. I can't believe you know her.

ATALANTA: Oh we go way back to my hippie-dippie days. I can't believe you still haven't met her.

ARISTAEUS: He guards her like a prized possession. What's she like?

ATALANTA: She's very simple. She's a wood nymph.

ARISTAEUS: So what does he see in her? Guy can have any girl he wants.

ATALANTA: Oh, don't get me wrong, she's great.

ARISTAEUS: So what's she like?

ATALANTA: She lives in the woods and stuff.

ARISTAEUS: Uh-huh.

ATALANTA: She's just not what you think of when you think of what hangs on the arm of a rock star.

ARISTAEUS: Can you believe they're talking marriage already?

ATALANTA: Since day one. I don't know. She says she loves him. She knows.

ARISTAEUS: He says the same, but…it's not good for the tabloids. It's too fast. The fans?

ATALANTA: It is fast.

ARISTAEUS: Hey, why do you suppose they call loose women "fast"?

ATALANTA: Beats me.

ARISTAEUS: You're the fastest woman alive and you're a virgin. You are still a virgin?

ATALANTA: I have to be fast. If a man catches me, I'd have to marry him. No offense.

ARISTAEUS: And why are you so opposed to marriage, Atalanta?

(ATALANTA *looks at* ARISTAEUS.)

ATALANTA: Well…I guess I've just never found the right guy.

ARISTAEUS: You've raced hundreds of men, you can't tell me there wasn't one of them you liked.

ATALANTA: There really wasn't. You want to race?

ARISTAEUS: Yeah, right. Whoever wins you have to marry, and if they lose, you kill them? I mean, don't you think that's a little extreme?

ATALANTA: Well, maybe I just find men sort of… repulsive.

ARISTAEUS: Are you from Lesbos?

ATALANTA: You know I'm not.

ARISTAEUS: Did you find me repulsive?

ATALANTA: That was a long time ago.

ARISTAEUS: Answer the question.

(Pause)

ATALANTA: Why did you call me? What is this about?
What's up with you?

ARISTAEUS: My best friend's marrying a woman I
haven't met, I wanted to get some dirt on her. So if you
ever lost a race, you'd marry the winner. That is your
fate?

ATALANTA: Those are my terms.

ARISTAEUS: Why on earth would you make those your
terms?

ATALANTA: Look. I'm the fastest mortal alive. And
that's how I want to be remembered. How will
Eurydice be remembered? As the wood nymph who
married Orpheus. Period. Traditional mythology will
have little else to say about her. Well, I have my own
place in the history books to think about.

ARISTAEUS: I think it's just an excuse.

ATALANTA: What is?

ARISTAEUS: You're just scared because you don't
believe that anyone could ever love you enough.

ATALANTA: I don't think so.

ARISTAEUS: You don't think you're worth it.

ATALANTA: So why aren't you married?

ARISTAEUS: I would one day. If I felt…

ATALANTA: What?

ARISTAEUS: Like he does. Like I did.

ATALANTA: Well I don't want to live in someone else's shadow.

ARISTAEUS: And Eurydice does?

ATALANTA: Eurydice wants to be remembered as Orpheus' wife. That's the greatest legacy she can imagine.

ARISTAEUS: Because of the fame of being the wife of a rock star?

ATALANTA: No. She said that her name would become synonymous with love. To say "Orpheus and Eurydice" would be to invoke the greatest bond of all time. Like Romeo and Juliet or something. She said, "The strength of their passion would be so great that lovers for centuries would envy the depths of their union."

ARISTAEUS: She said this?

ATALANTA: Yes.

ARISTAEUS: How could she know these things?

ATALANTA: I don't know. It's kind of corny though, don't you think?

ARISTAEUS: It is kind of corny.

Scene Six
A POKER TABLE

(*Cards, chips, beer, cigars.* ORPHEUS, HERCULES, JASON, *and* ARISTAEUS *play.* ORPHEUS *bets big.*)

JASON: I'm out.

HERCULES: Out.

ARISTAEUS: You're bluffing. Call.

(ORPHEUS *turns over his cards.*)

ORPHEUS: Never doubt my sincerity.

(ORPHEUS *rakes in his winnings. Everyone re-antes.*
HERCULES *deals.*)

HERCULES: So, Orpheus.

ORPHEUS: Yeah?

HERCULES: The big day? Any final requests? Speak now.

ORPHEUS: No.

HERCULES: Nothing? No? This is where the evening ends? No last night of debauchery?

ORPHEUS: No.

HERCULES: No whores, strippers, old loves? One last fling? What's the point of being here?

ORPHEUS: Those days are gone. With Eurydice I feel so much more...I don't know, complete.

JASON: We do get to meet her at the wedding, right?

ORPHEUS: Of course.

HERCULES: Well then...to the man who saved our asses by outplaying the Sirens and breaking the spell.

ARISTAEUS: And who brought beautiful music to a whole new generation of fans.

JASON: May the strength of your love endure.

HERCULES: May the courage of your conviction empower.

ARISTAEUS: And may her nymphish wiles take you to hell and back.

(*They drink.*)

HERCULES: How many?

ORPHEUS: Huh? Oh, I'm out.

HERCULES: You?

ARISTAEUS: Two.

HERCULES: Jason?

JASON: Three.

HERCULES: Dealer takes three.

JASON: *(To* ORPHEUS*)* So who's doing the ceremony?

ORPHEUS: Teiresias.

HERCULES: Old, blind freak.

JASON: Will you be nice?

ORPHEUS: It's a weird ceremony though. Wood nymphs do it weird, and I'm not allowed to see her until after I've said my vows.

HERCULES: They don't want you looking at her and deciding at the last minute she's not enough of a fox.

ORPHEUS: I just wish I could look into her eyes. She smiles with her eyes. It makes me feel…what's the word…?

HERCULES: So how do you like making it with a wood nymph? Wood nymphs are wild.

ORPHEUS: Eurydice's different.

HERCULES: Uh-huh. Right. I gotta get me another one of those.

ORPHEUS: You're married.

HERCULES: Whatever.

ARISTAEUS: Well I'll tell you one thing, I'm never getting married. Ten.

JASON: Ten? Too rich for my blood.

ORPHEUS: Of course you will.

ARISTAEUS: Not me. No way. Give me freedom or give me death. *(He drinks.)*

ORPHEUS: You just haven't found the right person.

JASON: How do you know Eurydice's the right person?

ORPHEUS: It feels right. The person I am when I'm with her, she just looks at me and I become better, I know it sounds...

HERCULES: Oh please. She's a nymph. Call.

JASON: Hercules.

HERCULES: What? She's not a nymph? You're a victim of nympholepsy. And believe me, after awhile it wears off. I mean, don't get me wrong, I love Daenaria and everything, but I'm a big man. I got big appetites.

ARISTAEUS, JASON, ORPHEUS: *(Overlapping)* Big appetites.

HERCULES: She just can't fulfill my every need. It's not realistic. Sometimes a man's gotta stray. And believe me, in the end, it's the best thing for the both of you.

ARISTAEUS: Most people just decide to settle down. Give up. There is no right person.

ORPHEUS: It's not like that.

HERCULES: She's perfect?

ORPHEUS: No, of course not. She has her flaws.

ARISTAEUS: Like what?

ORPHEUS: Well, you know, she's very simple. She could live in the woods forever and be happy. She's only moving to Thrace because of me. It's probably the thing we fight about the most.

HERCULES: So she's not perfect.

ORPHEUS: I don't think perfect means flawless. But she is the one for me. I know she is.

JASON: Here, here. *(He drinks.)*

HERCULES: "You know she is"? My hairy ass you do. Look at Oedipus. He "knew" too, right? And where did he end up? His fucking mother? Poor blind bastard.

JASON: Lay off him. It's the night before his wedding.

HERCULES: I'm just saying you don't know. Do you? You're just guessing. That's all.

JASON: This is supposed to be a celebration.

HERCULES: Guess all you want, and hey, I hope you guess right, I want nothing but happiness for you buddy, you know that. Just don't say you know, it's insulting.

ORPHEUS: Yeah? Well, I do.

ARISTAEUS: Three kings, what've you got?

HERCULES: You don't. You're as lost as the rest of us.

ORPHEUS: I have faith.

HERCULES: Yesterday's faith is today's fable.

ORPHEUS: No, it's more than that.

HERCULES: Faith is a bet. That's all it ever can be.

ARISTAEUS: What have you got?

HERCULES: What?

ARISTAEUS: What have you got?

HERCULES: (Showing his cards) I don't got dick.

Scene Seven
THE WEDDING CEREMONY OF ORPHEUS AND EURYDICE

(There is a podium center and next to it two large unlit torches and a central flame holder. ORPHEUS *stands waiting. Perhaps other characters are there as guests. Wedding music plays. After a beat* ARISTAEUS *enters and takes his place next to* ORPHEUS.*)*

ORPHEUS: Have you seen her? How does she look?

ARISTAEUS: I haven't seen her.

(A ruckus is heard offstage. TEIRESIAS *comes bursting into the theater. He is inexcusably late [not to mention blind].)*

TEIRESIAS: Thesuis, Thespius, Thesprotus! I'm so… excuse me, where's Orpheus? *(Feeling his face)* Ah, there you are my boy. My deepest apologies. This traffic. And these chariot drivers are crazy. And what's with these recordings? "Hello, this is Icarus. Chariots are much safer than wings made of wax, but please buckle your seat belt anyway. Don't fly too high, now." Gimme a break. Are we all set?

ARISTAEUS: We're waiting for Eurydice.

ORPHEUS: I'm not allowed to see her until after I've said my vows. She's here.

ARISTAEUS: She's not here. I think you're getting stood up.

ORPHEUS: She's here. Trust me, she's here.

ARISTAEUS: There's a difference between you not being allowed to see her, and her not being here.

TEIRESIAS: Is everything alright?

ORPHEUS: Everything's fine.

TEIRESIAS: We do seem to be missing something.

ORPHEUS: Just proceed, please.

TEIRESIAS: Oh right, that weird wood nymph thing. We are here today to join in holy matrimony Orpheus, son of Apollo and Calliope, and Eurydice, a wood nymph about whom traditional mythology tells us very little. Orpheus.

ARISTAEUS: Orpheus...

ORPHEUS: It's alright. She can hear me. *(He speaks as if* EURYDICE *were standing right next to him.)* Eurydice, since the moment I first heard your voice, I have wanted to live every moment next to you and end my days by your side. You are my muse and my poetry, my love and my breath. You are the thoughts in my head and the blood in my veins, the first thought of my day and the last image in my mind's eye before I sleep. With you I am alive and each day is a celebration of our love. I choose to grow old with you and become young again. I will love you, honor you, and die for you.

TEIRESIAS: Very good. Very lovely. Now Eurydice's vows are up next. But first Orpheus will light the holy torch as a symbol of the continuance of love. Eurydice, assuming she's here, will say her vows and add her flame so that the joined fire may burn eternally in your hearts as brightly as it does on the torch.

(ORPHEUS *lights one of the torches and then uses it to light the central flame holder. It sparks, flutters, and lets out a palish green smoke. There are screams of terror. Blackout)*

Scene Eight
A STUDIO

(ANDREA *appears in a spotlight. Behind her is a slide [a fire, a promo shot of* ORPHEUS, *etc.])*

ANDREA: Hi everyone, this is Andrea Siffolopolous for N T V news. The Thracian fire department received quite a shock today when it learned that the three-alarm fire it was fighting was the result of a bad omen that interrupted a secret marriage ceremony of the rock star Orpheus. No one was hurt in the fire and the ceremony was completed in a small affair in Vegas shortly afterwards. Speculation is now running wild as to what effect Orpheus' marriage will have on the follow-up to In Your Thrace's brilliant debut album and reporters are falling down over themselves to get more information on Orpheus' new bride, Eurydice, a wood nymph about whom traditional mythology tells us very little. We will bring you more information as it becomes available. And now back to the Real Underworld...

Scene Nine
SISYPHUS AND TANTALUS IN THE
UNDERWORLD

(SISYPHUS *is on a seesaw. He stands on one end so he is on the ground with the other end in the air. He has a large boulder which he pushes slowly up the seesaw as if to get it to stay at the top.)*

(TANTALUS *is treading water in a translucent box similar to the type at carnivals where you throw a ball and someone gets dunked. He can bite at the air around him, but can never touch his face to the water that surrounds him. He is facing in such a way that he cannot see* SISYPHUS.)

SISYPHUS: Fuck this rock is heavy.

TANTALUS: Keep pushing.

SISYPHUS: Uuugh!

TANTALUS: You can do it.

SISYPHUS: Aaaarrghh!

TANTALUS: Don't lose faith.

SISYPHUS: I can do it.

TANTALUS: That's better.

SISYPHUS: I have faith.

TANTALUS: Hang in there, Sisyphus buddy.

SISYPHUS: Jesus, I'm gonna need more than faith.

TANTALUS: Say…you got anything to drink?

SISYPHUS: Huh?

TANTALUS: I'm parched.

SISYPHUS: I don't think I do.

TANTALUS: Really? I mean I am quite seriously thirsty.

SISYPHUS: Almost there.

TANTALUS: I have never been so damn thirsty.

SISYPHUS: Uuuummph.

TANTALUS: Please, Sisyphus. Something to drink. I
implore you.

SISYPHUS: Just let me get this rock up to the top O K?
Just hang in there Tantalus.

(HOMELESSIUS *enters, counting change.*)

HOMELESSIUS: I'm sorry to interrupt. My wife and I
just got thrown out of a shelter and I'm trying to come
up with enough money to feed my three children. I
hate asking for money like this but I don't do drugs
and I want you to remember that this could happen
to anyone at any time. I just need twenty-five more

cents to have enough for a shelter. A nickel, a drachma, anything you could spare would really help me out.

SISYPHUS: Uh, yeah, here I think I have some change. Hang on a second.

(With great effort SISYPHUS rests the rock on his shoulder and digs out some coins which he gives to HOMELESSIUS.)

HOMELESSIUS: Oh, thank you. Twenty cents. Almost there. So close.

(HOMELESSIUS goes over to TANTALUS. TANTALUS treads water frantically and retrieves some coins which he tosses to HOMELESSIUS.)

TANTALUS: Un, yeah Homelessius, here you go.

HOMELESSIUS: Five cents, that's...that's twenty-five. That's perfect. Let's see, I've got five plus another ten, two bills with my quarters and that adds up to, oh, plus this twenty-five so I've got...da da da. No! No! I'm still twenty-five cents short you fiendish Gods of the Underworld! *(He exits, muttering his contempt.)*

TANTALUS: Tough break. Poor guy.

SISYPHUS: That really is Hell, isn't it?

TANTALUS: So, how are you doing with that damn rock?

SISYPHUS: I'll be with you in just a minute.

TANTALUS: Well hurry it up, damn it.

SISYPHUS: I'm doing my best.

TANTALUS: I'm really pretty fucking thirsty.

SISYPHUS: Why don't you just drink some of that water?

TANTALUS: What water?

SISYPHUS: That water you're swimming in.

TANTALUS: Huh? Oh, hey, good idea. *(He gasps furiously for the water but he can only bite air. He thrashes*

*about desperately trying to catch some of the water in his
mouth but it is to no avail.)* Oh you cursed Gods of
the Underworld, you surround me in the promise of
salvation but deliver me with none. I hate you, I hate
you. This is tantalizing.

SISYPHUS: Hang in there, Tantalus, I'm coming, I've
almost got it. Uuungh.

*(He reaches the top of the seesaw which tips it. He finds
himself at the bottom on the other side looking up at what is
now the new top of his "hill". TANTALUS cannot see him.)*

TANTALUS: Well…? Did you get it to the top? Good
work buddy. Knew you could do it. Now, please, I'm
dying of thirst over here.

SISYPHUS: Um…., I'll be there in just a minute, 'K?

Scene Ten
TEIRESIAS'S DEN OF PROPHECY

(TEIRESIAS sits as ORPHEUS enters his chamber.)

ORPHEUS: Thank you for seeing me, Teiresias.

TEIRESIAS: I am a busy old oracle, but this situation calls
for guidance. Sit down.

*(ORPHEUS sits. TEIRESIAS stretches out his arms to "lay
hands" on ORPHEUS but, being blind, he gropes around a
bit.)*

TEIRESIAS: Well, where the Hades are you boy? Give an
old blind oracle a break.

ORPHEUS: Sorry.

(ORPHEUS leans his head into TEIRESIAS's hands.)

TEIRESIAS: That's better.

(TEIRESIAS *holds* ORPHEUS's *head, his thumbs over*
ORPHEUS's *closed eyes.* TEIRESIAS *moans and whirs like a*
man possessed, then he breaks free.)

ORPHEUS: What have you seen?

TEIRESIAS: Um...I hate giving bad news. Are you sure
you wouldn't rather I make a prediction about the
Knicks? *(Or substitute your local failing sports team)*

ORPHEUS: It's hard to imagine a prediction about the
Knicks would be good news.

TEIRESIAS: Good point. Alright. The sputtering of
the wedding torch is a terribly bad omen. It signals
unhappiness and misfortune. But here is what I have
seen inside your eyes: your marriage displeases the
Gods and is doomed. It can end only in misery and
death.

ORPHEUS: Why?

TEIRESIAS: It is not ours to ask why.

ORPHEUS: Are you saying I should annul the marriage?

TEIRESIAS: No...

ORPHEUS: Because that would be the saddest fate of all.
But as long as we're together I have nothing to fear.

TEIRESIAS: If you say so. Everyone's a prophet.
Orpheus, listen...

ORPHEUS: There must be a way to beat this prophecy.
We can overcome their obstacles because we have each
other.

TEIRESIAS: Orpheus, listen to me! It doesn't matter what
you do. You cannot escape your destiny.

ORPHEUS: Everyone says my music is a gift from the
Gods, that it pleases them, but now they are jealous of
our love and want to punish us for it.

TEIRESIAS: The Gods are not j...

ORPHEUS: Well instead I'll punish them. I'll break up the band.

TEIRESIAS: You can't escape your d...

ORPHEUS: If that's what it takes, I defy the Gods, I defy the prophecy, and I renounce the band. Eurydice is more important than the band. She's all there is and all there ever will be.

Scene Eleven
ORPHEUS'S PLACE

(ORPHEUS *is packing.*)

ARISTAEUS: You can't do this.

ORPHEUS: I can.

ARISTAEUS: Big O, think of the fans.

ORPHEUS: What about them?

ARISTAEUS: They'll be devastated.

ORPHEUS: I don't care.

ARISTAEUS: The band?

ORPHEUS: They'll understand.

ARISTAEUS: Hercules is going to understand?

ORPHEUS: He'll have to.

ARISTAEUS: This band is everything to him. If you take it away...

ORPHEUS: I just need to talk to them. Next week after I'm settled into the new place with Eurydice.

ARISTAEUS: What about the Gods?

ORPHEUS: This isn't about the Gods...

ARISTAEUS: Not about the...

ORPHEUS: ...I just don't want to do this anymore.

ARISTAEUS: Orpheus. Listen to me. Fame is confusing.
Everyone wants something from you. So allow me to
make a recommendation. Trust your friends. Trust
the people who have been there for you. We are
Argonauts, damnit! Does that mean nothing to you
anymore? After The Golden Fleece, the Sirens, that
whole fucking trip!? And then some fucking wood
nymph comes along—

ORPHEUS: She's my wife.

ARISTAEUS: I don't care who she is. She says she loves
you and you throw away the greatest thing that ever
happened to you?

ORPHEUS: She does love me.

ARISTAEUS: Maybe she does. The question is why.
Love is fake. Love is a tool to get what you want. She
wants something from you. Money? A taste of fame.
Whatever. You barely know her.

ORPHEUS: Fuck you. I know her. How dare you?

ARISTAEUS: O K, I'm sorry. Look, I understand. Believe
me. You need an anchor. You are washed out to sea,
floating on a wave of faceless fans. I understand this.
But she is the wrong anchor. It's as clear as day to
everyone but you. They may not say it to your face, but
believe me they are saying it behind your back. Let me
be your anchor. Your friends, we'll take care of you.

ORPHEUS: I'm not turning my back on my friends. Why
are you taking this personally?

ARISTAEUS: Because it is personal. Sometimes you just
can't see for yourself and you need help. Why won't
you let me help?

ORPHEUS: You can help, you just can't stop me from
doing what I know is right. I see everything much
more clearly than I ever did. I never liked that life.

ARISTAEUS: With the band?

ORPHEUS: No.

ARISTAEUS: On the boat?

ORPHEUS: On the boat it was different. I just did it and it saved lives. Now it's what? It just makes a bunch of screaming kids dance.

ARISTAEUS: But that's good.

ORPHEUS: It's not good enough.

ARISTAEUS: To get someone out of their skin for a few minutes? To give them pleasure? To help them forget their miserable lives? Think about your favorite song. How much it means to you. To give someone that?

ORPHEUS: It's not from my soul. The music has become a commercial to buy a product called Orpheus.

ARISTAEUS: And she's not pressuring you in any way?

ORPHEUS: No. When I sing for her I make music. When I sing for them I make...

ARISTAEUS: Money. But the fact that you make money does not make what you do evil. It does not. Look, I'm your friend. The best you've got. And I can see how happy she makes you, and that makes me happy. But let me ask you this: how do you know she truly loves you? How do you know she'll be there for you? Stand behind you?

ORPHEUS: Because I choose to have one hundred percent faith.

ARISTAEUS: There's no such thing. Faith implies doubt. By definition.

ORPHEUS: You don't understand it because you don't have it. Look, how did I know I could outplay the Sirens? How did I know, know, we'd return with the Golden Fleece? I know things because I believe them.

And I'll tell you: I have never, never, in all my life known anything as strongly as this. I'd do anything for her. Anything.

Scene Twelve
A STUDIO

(ANDREA *appears in a spotlight. Behind her is a slide [In Your Thrace in the studio or something]. She sits in a studio with* JASON *and* HERCULES.)

ANDREA: Hi everyone, this is Andrea Siffolopolous for N T V news. And have we got a major thrill for you. Live in our studios, Jason and Hercules from In Your Thrace.

JASON: Hey Andrea.

HERCULES: What's up?

ANDREA: So where's Orpheus?

JASON: What's the matter, we're not good enough for you?

ANDREA: Well, he is the lead singer of the band.

HERCULES: He's off...you know, writing songs.

ANDREA: I don't think you've ever given an interview without Orpheus.

HERCULES: Uh...I don't know.

JASON: Who can remember? We've done so many, right?

ANDREA: This doesn't signal any bad blood does it?

HERCULES: What are you, Barbara Walters?

JASON: Of course it doesn't.

ANDREA: Really?

HERCULES: We're just here to...

JASON: In Your Thrace is as healthy as it's ever been.

ANDREA: Because I don't know if the world could handle the band breaking up.

JASON: The band is not breaking up.

HERCULES: The band is definitely not breaking up.

(ANDREA *turns to address the audience.*)

ANDREA: You heard it here first folks. Major tensions in the band In Your Thrace, and a strong possibility that the band is breaking up.

Scene Thirteen
THE NEW HOME OF ORPHEUS AND EURYDICE

(ARISTAEUS *and* ATALANTA *are carrying in boxes through the front door.*)

ATALANTA: O K. This is the last one.

ARISTAEUS: Thanks a lot for helping with the move.

ATALANTA: That's what friends do.

ARISTAEUS: I know they appreciate it.

ATALANTA: My pleasure.

ARISTAEUS: Wait a minute. Oh shit. Where's that plant? Did you grab it?

ATALANTA: They want that plant?

ARISTAEUS: She's a wood nymph.

ATALANTA: Right. No big deal. Hang on. *(She exits. Returns immediately with the plant.)*

ARISTAEUS: Show off.

ATALANTA: If you've got it, flaunt it.

ARISTAEUS: But don't flaunt what you're not prepared
to use.

ATALANTA: Oh get over it, look I gotta get going.
I'm late for a race.

ARISTAEUS: You late?

ATALANTA: Ha ha ha.

ARISTAEUS: Eurydice was right behind us, you're not
going to stick around and say goodbye?

ATALANTA: No, I gotta go. Say goodbye for me.

ARISTAEUS: Whatever.

(ATALANTA *exits.* ARISTAEUS *goes over to a mirror [or
a pretend mirror or something]. Practices. N B: the actor
playing* ARISTAEUS *should not allow a realistic amount of
time for the "pretend"* EURYDICE *he is practicing with to
answer.)*

ARISTAEUS: Eurydice, hey, let me help you with that.
(He crosses to the door. Back to the mirror) Eurydice, that
looks heavy, need a hand? *(He crosses to the door. Back
to the mirror)* Oh, hey, let me get that. *(He crosses to the
door. Back to the mirror)* So how's married life treating
you? Uh huh. Yeah. No, I know, because he sure
seems nuts about you too. Yeah. Almost too nuts if
you know what I mean. I mean has Orpheus written
any new songs lately? He has? That's great. But can I
hear them? No, he only wants to play them for you?
Well don't you think that's a little weird? I mean why
won't he share his songs? No, his heart isn't in the
band, his heart is with you. Well that's a little selfish.
I think that's a bit of a problem don't you? You don't?
I do. Don't you? You don't? No, hey, don't go. Come
on, hey, where are you going? Get back in here. Get
back in here I said! *(He readjusts. Doesn't like how angry
he's becoming. Tries a lighter touch)* I mean, think of the
fans, you know? That's all I really care about. They're

being deprived of Orpheus's genius. And for what?
Why? He has a responsibility to weave his magic.
And I, I guess, am a guardian of that power. A keeper
of that flame. It's my responsibility to see to it that
Orpheus does his job. Does that make sense to you?
No? Eurydice, be reasonable. I'm being reasonable
with you. I just want you to talk to him, see if you can
get him to…You fucking bitch! You stupid cunt you're
ruining everything! (He readjusts. Doesn't like how
frustrated he's become. Tries flattery) Eurydice you are a
lucky woman. You know how many women would
kill to be in your shoes? I mean, you are the envy of
the entire female population. So play ball with me, O
K? Talk to Orpheus. Get him to give up this crazy talk
about breaking up the band. I mean A, think of him.
It's not going to make him happy. Not ultimately, you
know that. B, think of the fans. Obvious. But most
importantly is C. Think of you. The band breaking
up is, after all, all your fault as far as the fans are
concerned and they will crucify you. You don't want
that. I don't want that. Certainly Orpheus doesn't
want that. You're not a villain. Bitch! You fucking
bitch! You're just in the way and that's all there is to it.
Things were so much better before you came along!

(Suddenly the front door opens though we cannot see what's
behind it. ARISTAEUS is shocked, then quickly regains his
composure.)

ARISTAEUS: Eurydice, you scared me, oh hey let me get
that.

(He crosses towards the door. Blackout)

ACT ONE   37

Scene Fourteen
THE NEW HOME OF ORPHEUS AND
EURYDICE

(It is a short time later. DEATH, *a beautiful though somewhat freakish woman, stands onstage. She is accompanied by two assistants who carry clipboards.)*

DEATH: It stinks in here. Foul air.

#2: Who's next?

#1: *(Consulting a clipboard)* Eurydice.

#2: No.

#1: What it says here.

#2: The wood nymph who married Orpheus?

#1: I guess.

#2: The one about whom traditional mythology tells us very little?

#1: That's the one.

#2: Are we gonna run into him? Think he'll give us an autograph?

DEATH: Children… we have work to do.

(#1 opens a suitcase and removes some complicated-looking electronic equipment.)

DEATH: It seems such a shame to take her. Someone so young. Cut down in her prime. Oh well, them's the breaks. *(She points offstage.)*

DEATH: She's in there. Hook up her soul.

(#2 pulls a line from the equipment offstage to EURYDICE. *The line remains taut and suspended above the ground. Occasionally it quivers.)*

#1: Um…

DEATH: Yes?

#1: We uh, forgot something.

DEATH: Our signature book?

#1: *(Pointing to his clipboard)* Nope. Got that. Signatures of the dead all in tow.

DEATH: What then?

#1: Our time-stopper. No big deal. It just means we have to move quickly.

DEATH: I don't like being rushed, Number One.

#1: Sorry.

DEATH: Use your watch.

#1: I don't have a watch.

DEATH: Number Two?

#2: Don't have one.

DEATH: You don't have a watch? How do you know what time it is?

#2: Well, um, we're like dead and stuff so we don't really care.

DEATH: We need a time piece.

#1: O K, I'll see what I can do. *(She goes into the audience until she gets a watch. She attaches the watch to the equipment.)*

DEATH: In the end I suppose it doesn't matter. Time doesn't move through us. Time remains. Still as stone. We move through it.

#1: I believe we're ready.

DEATH: O K, I'll go get her soul. *(Exits)*

#2: Dude, un-stop time.

#1: What? Why?

#2: I want to meet Orpheus.

#1: We can't do that.

#2: You heard what she said, "Time doesn't move through us," blah blah blah.

#1: I wouldn't make fun of Death like that.

#2: Why not? What's she going to do? "Kill me?" Look. Just say it's `cause of the watch. It's not our fault, it's his. *(Points to the person who gave up the watch)*

#1: Now that's not very nice, you want Death mad at him?

#2: I don't care, everybody's got to go sometime. Here, I'll do it.

(#2 starts fiddling with the equipment. DEATH *returns, carrying a white dove.)*

DEATH: Her soul. So pure. So clean. So mine.

(She puts the dove in a cage. #1 begins to put the equipment away.)

DEATH: How are we on the rest of the night?

#1: Well, there was a fairly big skirmish in the Trojan War so we're gonna have to go pick up some souls over there.

DEATH: Let's get moving.

#2: We sure we're not forgetting anything?

DEATH: Like what?

#2: Oh I don't know. I just think we should be sure.

DEATH: Do we have everything?

#1: I think we're all set. *(To #2)* Sorry. Don't get to meet Orpheus.

#2: Damn.

DEATH: What's wrong with you?

#2: Nothing. Oh! What about that guy's watch?

DEATH: Oh yes. Return the kind gentleman's watch.

(#1 *goes into the audience to return the watch. From offstage we hear a chariot pulling up and the following voice over: "Hi, this is Narcissus again. I sure am great. Don't forget your belongings or your receipt. Have a day as good as me." Followed by Jason's voice.*)

JASON: *(O S)* You want me to start putting stuff inside?

DEATH: Oh my. Should've kept time stopped for awhile longer. Hide, everyone.

(DEATH *takes a seat in the audience. #1 exits. #2 looks around and hides somewhere obvious.*)

Scene Fifteen
THE NEW HOME OF ORPHEUS AND EURYDICE

(*A continuation.* JASON *enters, carrying a large mirror.*)

JASON: Where should I put this mirror?

ORPHEUS: *(O S)* Hang it over there.

(JASON *hangs the mirror as* HERCULES *and* ORPHEUS *enter, carrying boxes.* ORPHEUS *is struggling with his.*)

ORPHEUS: Damn this is heavy.

HERCULES: Allow me. (*He takes the box and easily adds it to his already overbearing load.*)

ORPHEUS: Thanks big guy. Eurydice! We're back.

(HERCULES *discovers Assistant #2.*)

HERCULES: Hey. Who are you?

#2: Oh, uh, I was just hoping for Orpheus' autograph.

HERCULES: Jesus Christ. You've got some nerve. You think you can just break into someone's house and…?

JASON: Get the hell out of here.

(HERCULES *goes over to manhandle #2.*)

ORPHEUS: No, no, it's O K.

(#2 holds out the clipboard and a pen for ORPHEUS *to sign.)*

#2: Oh, thanks, man. I really appreciate it.

ORPHEUS: Who should I make it out to?

#2: Two.

ORPHEUS: To two? *(He starts to sign.)*

#2: No that's T-W-O.

ORPHEUS: Here you go.

#2: No! Wait! Don't sign there. Here.

*(*ORPHEUS *signs.)*

#2: It's really good to see the three of you together. I mean, I heard rumors the band was breaking up.

HERCULES & JASON: The band is not breaking up.

#2: Dude, right on. So the band's gonna stay together!

ORPHEUS: Hey, who are all these names?

#2: Oh, just people.

ORPHEUS: What's my wife's name doing here?

#2: Uh…

ORPHEUS: Huh?

#2: I gotta go. Thanks for the autograph. *(He bolts.)*

JASON: What the fuck was that?

ORPHEUS: Eurydice! Eurydice!? Where'd she go?

JASON: I'll check in here. *(He exits.)*

HERCULES: Creep. Hey, what's that smell?

ORPHEUS: What?

HERCULES: You don't smell it?

ORPHEUS: No.

HERCULES: It smells like death.

(JASON *reenters.*)

JASON: Oh God.

ORPHEUS: What's wrong?

JASON: It's…

ORPHEUS: What?

(ORPHEUS *starts to go for the door but* HERCULES *stops him.*)

JASON: Don't go in there.

ORPHEUS: Why? What's wrong?

JASON: Here. Look through this. (*He points to the mirror.*)

ORPHEUS: Why can't I see?

JASON: Your eyes should not see such a thing directly.

(ORPHEUS *looks. The mirror becomes opaque like a screen and onto it is projected a film of* EURYDICE. *We do not see her face. The film is black and white, scratchy like from a different time. We see* EURYDICE *lying still. Dead*)

ORPHEUS: EURYDICE!

(*The lights change. The film starts moving.*)

EURYDICE: (*V O on film*) Orpheus. Orpheus, help me. Save me. Return me from the Underworld.

(*The film cuts and repeats like that Princess Leia thing in Star Wars ["Help me Obi-Wan-Kanobe, you're my only hope."].*)

ORPHEUS: Oh my God. Eurydice no. Eurydice. No.

(DEATH *steps out of her hiding place and laughs as only Death can. Blackout*)

END OF ACT ONE

ACT TWO

Scene Sixteen
A STUDIO

(ANDREA *appears in a spotlight. Behind her is a slide* [ORPHEUS *pushing a cameraman out of the way à la Sean Penn and Madonna.* ORPHEUS's *hand allows the camera to glimpse* EURYDICE, *but we cannot see her face].*)

ANDREA: Hi everyone, this is Andrea Siffolopolous for N T V news and we have some late-breaking news just in. Apparently Orpheus's bride Eurydice has died. An unconfirmed early report is that she was poisoned when she stepped on a snake. Since their wedding, jealous fans have been desperate for a peek at her but this is the closest glimpse of Eurydice anyone has been able to capture. We are just getting information on this late-breaking development and obviously we will bring you more information as it becomes available. Now back to N T V's Spring Break Babe Freak-Out Fest.

Scene Seventeen
THE NEW HOME OF ORPHEUS AND
EURYDICE

(ORPHEUS *and* ARISTAEUS)

ARISTAEUS: It was a very good service. Even laying there dead she still looked so beautiful.

ORPHEUS: I don't…I just don't understand how it could have happened. It was my music.

ARISTAEUS: What?

ORPHEUS: My music must have killed her.

ARISTAEUS: Orpheus, don't talk crazy. Your music is a gift. Your music pleases the Gods. Playing your music can only lead to good things.

ORPHEUS: You saw her last. How…what kind of a state was she in? Please. Explain it to me again, I just don't get it.

ARISTAEUS: Why do you keep wanting to go through it?

ORPHEUS: I want to understand.

ARISTAEUS: Atalanta left. I kept doing some unpacking. Eurydice came home. She and I talked. She went outside to bring in more stuff, and she stepped on a snake which bit her. I heard her scream, ran outside, brought her to her bed. I ran to get help, and that's when you guys showed up.

ORPHEUS: Well…what did you two talk about? What were her last words?

ARISTAEUS: I don't think I should say.

ORPHEUS: Tell me.

ARISTAEUS: We had a very strange conversation.

ORPHEUS: Tell me.

ARISTAEUS: I really don't think I should…

ORPHEUS: Tell me.

ARISTAEUS: Well, she was in a lot of pain, and she was quite dizzy and nauseous. She must've known she was dying. And she said, "Don't tell him, don't tell Orpheus". And I said, "Don't tell him what?" And she said, "Don't tell him the truth." And then she was out.

ORPHEUS: The truth about what?

ARISTAEUS: I don't know.

ORPHEUS: I'm scared.

ARISTAEUS: Of the truth?

ORPHEUS: Of going on without her.

ARISTAEUS: It won't be easy. It'll take some time, but...

ORPHEUS: Can I ask you a question?

ARISTAEUS: Of course.

ORPHEUS: It's horrible.

ARISTAEUS: What? Anything?

ORPHEUS: And don't lie to me, no matter how bad it is, O K?

ARISTAEUS: Sure.

ORPHEUS: Well some people are saying...that you killed her.

ARISTAEUS: What!?

ORPHEUS: Did you?

ARISTAEUS: I am your best friend. If you don't have faith in me, what can you have faith...?

ORPHEUS: Just look me in the eye and tell me.

(ARISTAEUS *looks* ORPHEUS *square in the eye.*)

ARISTAEUS: Orpheus. I didn't kill her.

(ORPHEUS *breaks away, crying.*)

ARISTAEUS: How could you think…?

ORPHEUS: I'm sorry.

ARISTAEUS: It's O K.

ORPHEUS: I'm so confused.

ARISTAEUS: It's alright.

ORPHEUS: People say things. Plant doubts, it's like poison. Poisonous thoughts.

ARISTAEUS: It's forgiven. Look, I know you're in an incredible amount of pain. But great pain can lead to the great things.

ORPHEUS: Never again.

ARISTAEUS: What do you mean?

ORPHEUS: I'm finished with music. Without Eurydice there is no music.

ARISTAEUS: Don't say that.

ORPHEUS: Without Eurydice I'm through.

Scene Eighteen/Scene Nineteen
THE UNDERWORLD/THE NEW HOME OF
ORPHEUS AND EURYDICE

(DEATH *strokes a white dove as* ORPHEUS *sits in his house crying and drinking. They do connect with each other.*)

DEATH: Hello my pretty little soul. Yes. Cooey. Cooey.

ORPHEUS: Eurydice?

DEATH: I can see the passion still throbbing hot inside you.

ORPHEUS: Eurydice?

DEATH: Someone misses you very much I'm sure.

ORPHEUS: I love you.

DEATH: But now it's time for you to move beyond all that and choose how you will spend eternity.

ORPHEUS: I miss you.

DEATH: Eternity is a long time deary...

ORPHEUS: I love you.

DEATH: So choose a labor that will sate your soul such that wild horses couldn't drag you away.

ORPHEUS: Don't die. Don't be dead.

DEATH: Choose and set yourself free.

(DEATH *goes to throw the dove into the air as if to set it free. The dove vanishes. We hear the sound of fluttering wings as* DEATH *exits. The wings get louder and more ominous and they mix with the sound of white noise, guitar feedback.* ORPHEUS *tries to run and hide from the sound.* ORPHEUS *screams as if his screams could make the sound stop. He picks up his guitar and goes to smash it. As the guitar would "hit" a blast of light and screeching sound. He "smashes" the guitar several times, each time causing the overall noise to build. The building of the sound takes awhile.* ORPHEUS *rails against the sound, screaming.*)

ORPHEUS: No! Please! Stay away from me! Stay Away From Me! Eurydice! Eurydice! I love you.

(*Shadows of wings and flickers of light descend on him. The screaming, lights, and sound reach a peak of cacophonous madness. Then sudden silence and dark.*)

Scene Twenty
THE NEW HOME OF ORPHEUS AND EURYDICE

(HERCULES *and* ARISTAEUS *stand over* ORPHEUS, *who wakes with a jump. The bottle of alcohol is present.*)

ORPHEUS: Argh!

HERCULES: Orpheus, are you alright?

ARISTAEUS: Orpheus, it was a dream. You were dreaming.

ORPHEUS: What? All of it? Is she alive? Did I meet her?

HERCULES: Orpheus, listen.

ORPHEUS: It's real, it's all real. I know it's real.

ARISTAEUS: Orpheus, it's been seven months. You've barely moved. You've cried a river. Now, I know these things take time, but you've got to start taking some steps.

ORPHEUS: I miss her so much.

HERCULES: Why don't we go down to the studio and play some stuff? Just for fun.

ORPHEUS: I hear demons screaming in my ears and I can't make it stop.

HERCULES: Maybe you should go away for awhile. Find someone to talk to.

ARISTAEUS: No, you have to let us help you. You can't go on like this.

HERCULES: Just tell us what you need, buddy.

ORPHEUS: I need my wife back.

ARISTAEUS: What do you need that we can do for you?

(JASON *enters with* TEIRESIAS.)

ORPHEUS: What is he doing here?

JASON: I had an idea. I brought him here to help. We've talked and…

ORPHEUS: I don't want him here.

ARISTAEUS: Maybe you should go.

HERCULES: What's the idea?

TEIRESIAS: I am only a messenger. It is not me you hate.

JASON: Well…there may be a way.

TEIRESIAS: It probably won't work.

HERCULES: What?

ARISTAEUS: What are you talking about?

JASON: There could be a way to get her back.

ARISTAEUS: No.

ORPHEUS: How?

TEIRESIAS: Getting her back is not the issue.

ORPHEUS: Tell me.

TEIRESIAS: But if you wish, you can go to the Underworld and petition Death.

ARISTAEUS: What are you nuts?

ORPHEUS: Wh…what do you mean?

HERCULES: Are you out of your mind? No one has returned from the Underworld.

TEIRESIAS: That is true.

HERCULES: It's not an option.

TEIRESIAS: That is not true.

ORPHEUS: What would I do? How does it work?

TEIRESIAS: You can go through the mirror.

ARISTAEUS: Through the mirror?

HERCULES: It's too dangerous.

JASON: We're just presenting an option.

TEIRESIAS: Mirrors are portals to the Underworld. Stare into a mirror long enough and you'll see Death creep up and overtake you. Or you can go through.

ORPHEUS: How?

TEIRESIAS: Believe.

ORPHEUS: That's it?

TEIRESIAS: Believing is a lot harder than it sounds. If you get through, you'll have to pass three guards and then you'll be at the entrance to the Underworld.

HERCULES: Charon, Minos, and Cerberus.

TEIRESIAS: Very good. If you find Death you can make your case and attempt to strike a bargain with her to win Eurydice back.

ARISTAEUS: I've never heard of this.

HERCULES: That's because no one has successfully done it. Ever.

TEIRESIAS: That doesn't make it impossible.

JASON: No one thought we'd bring back the Golden Fleece either.

ORPHEUS: I have to try, right, I mean, even if there's only a slim hope…

HERCULES: Don't let your hubris be your downfall. You cannot accomplish this. You need to accept the facts of life, and let the dead be.

ARISTAEUS: Her being dead might be a good thing in the overall scheme of things.

HERCULES: You don't know. You cannot go against the natural order of the world.

ORPHEUS: No, what I cannot do is live without her. What I cannot do is go back to a life of sheepish fans who have blind faith in me for no reason.

HERCULES: But you have no right. You can't take it upon yourself to decide these things.

ARISTAEUS: How do you know we don't need you more?

HERCULES: How do you know she doesn't prefer being dead?

ORPHEUS: I know…because I know. Death isn't a good enough reason for me to stop loving her.

JASON: If it's what he wants to do you can't get in his way.

HERCULES: Don't tell me what I can't do.

JASON: Don't tell him what he can't do.

HERCULES: And will you drop that fucking accent?

JASON: What are you talking about?

HERCULES: It adds nothing.

(JASON *drops the accent.*)

JASON: Fine. Sorry.

HERCULES: Why are you doing this?

JASON: Because if there's one thing I learned on that quest, it's that love is stronger than the greatest force.

HERCULES: Bullshit. You want the band to break up. You just can't stomach taking a supporting role you little ego fuck.

JASON: What!?

HERCULES: Well you are not the leader anymore. The quest is over. Just because you assembled us…you know I was voted the leader. Unanimously. I let you do

ARISTAEUS: Why are you doing this?

TEIRESIAS: Jason asked for a favor, I'm doing him a favor.

ARISTAEUS: Bullshit. You want the band to break up. Teiresias, you can't let him do this.

TEIRESIAS: I can do what I please.

ARISTAEUS: You're sending a man, my friend, to his death. For what? To prove some prophecy? Please…

it because I didn't want
to hurt your…

JASON: You're bringing   TEIRESIAS: A prophecy's
that up again? Now?   a prophecy. How the
                                pieces fall into place
                                is irelevant.

HERCULES: Fuck you.   ARISTAEUS: Fuck you.

(ORPHEUS *crashes through the mirror and out of sight.*)

Scene Twenty-one
ORPHEUS IN THE UNDERWORLD

(*Projection: Orpheus in the Underworld*)

(*It is important for this scene that* ORPHEUS'*s voice be
amplified. Ideally he would wear a body mike that would now
be turned on. If possible, he should not hold a microphone,
though a "rock-star" styled headset would be appropriate.*)

(*This scene should have a very different feel to anything
we've seen so far. Underscoring of some sort and moody
light would be lovely. Some sound effects are suggested.*)

(ORPHEUS *is discovered in a shaft of light.*)

ORPHEUS: Teiresias has warned me of the three staunch
guards who I must face before allowed my entrance to
the Underworld. The first is Charon, boatman of the
river Styx.

(*The sound of wind over broken glass*)

ORPHEUS: Before my eyes I see a trail of spirits,
winding long and far. They wait to pay the old,
white-haired shuttler of souls. There are so many of
them, I'm aghast and overcome by just how fast cold
death removes our mortal coil. The souls await their
boarding call with all the patience and restraint of
those for whom eternity does beckon. But all my living

restlessness and hot ambition ring out like a warm-
blooded call to arms. And Charon becomes forced to
reckon with my need for entrance and deliverance.

CHARON: *(V O)* Woe to you wicked soul. Abandon all
thoughts of salvation! I am come to ferry you across
into eternal dark!

(The sound of an oar rhythmically parting flaming water)

ORPHEUS: And with that charge he grabs my mouth in
order to extract his fee: the deadman's coin residing
underneath the tongue of the departed. Realizing I'm
without my fare does give him pause, as he now sees
that I am still alive. Still he demands a payment for his
service. But then he looks and recognizes me. At least
he recognizes my celebrity. He says that he will ferry
me across. I do not have to pay if I just play for him a
song from my new album. Except I know that no such
song exists. But if I cannot find a way, then I am lost
without my love, and so to my surprise…

(Absolute silence)

ORPHEUS: I sing a song that I compose right there. And
when he hears the song he's instantly entranced, and
he agrees to ferry me across.

*(ORPHEUS moves to another side of the stage. The sound of a
claw scraping stone as gas fires ignite and whoosh.)*

ORPHEUS: Once safely shuttled to the dark side of the
river, my challenge now becomes a larger one. For
I must face one of the fierce and fetid judges of the
dead. Minos then steps out to challenge me, gnaring,
knocking, gnashing his black teeth. His sinister, spiked
tail tap-tap taps out thunder greedily as he anticipates
the revelation of my sins. He licks his lips just like
the connoisseur of the immoral that he is, voraciously
awaiting to devour my tales of wickedness. To
henceforth spit his vile judgment on my soul. But I

tell him my time has yet to come. And that I am but kicking at the doors to get in, to the very place where souls spend all eternity lamenting, howling, crying to get out.

(A human-hyena's laugh echoes out loudly in the caverny distance.)

ORPHEUS: He cackles at my foolishness, drools bile off his fangs and chastises my hubris. But I just sing to him a song.

(Absolute silence)

ORPHEUS: The lyrics seem to write themselves. My soul sings out the depth of my resolve. And when I'm done, the judge of sins relents, allowing me to pass.

(ORPHEUS moves again. The sound of a thousand rabid dogs scream and growl as one.)

ORPHEUS: My third and final challenge is now Cerberus, the vile three-headed dog beast, who stands guard, and ferociously forbids admittance to the dark and the obscur'ed underworld. Cerberus, whose very talons flay and quarter all the souls of the departed. Upon his seeing me he growls, snarls, and barks, with each of his repugnant heads more vicious, hideous, flagitious than the last. He smells the lifeblood in my veins and without mercy or remorse he seeks to rip my soul from me. I have no time to think or to react. I simply start to sing.

(Absolute silence)

ORPHEUS: His three heads cock back plaintively at me, as to suggest that he has never heard before such beauty. At once I'm stricken cold with pity for this beast, who's lived a thousand lifetimes but without his ever grazing the sublime. His eyes blink sorrowfully at me, he utters out a delicate, soft yelp. My melody has lulled the beast to sleep. *(He moves again.)* I've met

my three dark challenges and I've endured. And so
I'm filled with greater confidence. The gates into the
Underworld loom high above me, its message there
emblazoned final as the termination of our lives.

GATES: *(V O)* Through me you enter into the city
of woes. Through me you enter into eternal pain.
Through me you enter the population of loss. Abandon
all hope, you who enter here.

*(ORPHEUS moves again. The various sounds of the
Underworld continue to underscore.)*

ORPHEUS: And enter I do. With all the strengths of
my conviction at their peak, I burst right through the
gates with my demand: Eurydice should be returned
to me! But I am stopped dead-cold in my fresh tracks.
I am reduced to tears by the incogitable scope of
suffering that I can see and feel empathically as if it
were my own. All my defenses are dismissed, the
essence of my being is diminished to the core. I am
engulfed into a pitch black place without...hope. The
sighs, laments, and groans of tortured souls ring out—
deafening my ears. I'm overcome with wailing sounds
of woe that deaden the stale air, a thousand foreign
languages ring out in nauseating screams of rage
and agony. The sound of beating hands on flesh and
never-ending flailing mix with sounds of scratching
which pervades it all. Scratch and scratch and scratch
and scratch, the scaling and the scraping sounds as
millions upon millions of sick scabs are ripped from
flesh—the tearing, rashing grating of man's limbs—it
screeches out into the endless void that knows no time.
And as my eyes adjust to Godless dark, I see myself
surrounded now by swarming souls, mere shadows of
their old corporeal selves. The most grotesquely and
misshapen, contorted and deformed, existences that
my mind's eye could possibly imagine. And am I not
an Argonaut? I've seen the fiercest battles and the most

disgusting creatures. Yet nothing—yet no thing in my whole shallow life could possibly prepare me for these creatures of the damned. Gashes, gruesome gouges have replaced the severed limbs and men are torn wide open, with their wounds still steaming fresh and hot. Chests ripped wide from chin down to the ass and from the splayed old torso pour new bloody entrails hanging and still dripping, oozing gore down to the knees. Organs, stomachs, feces spurtle, dribble, gush from open wounds. *(Pause)* But enough. I think you get the idea.

Scene Twenty-two
SISYPHUS AND TANTALUS IN THE UNDERWORLD

(Back with SISYPHUS *and* TANTALUS. *Same as before)*

SISYPHUS: Fuck this rock is heavy.

TANTALUS: Keep pushing.

SISYPHUS: Uuugh!

TANTALUS: You can do it.

SISYPHUS: Aaaarrghh!

TANTALUS: Don't lose faith.

SISYPHUS: I can do it.

TANTALUS: That's better.

SISYPHUS: I have faith.

TANTALUS: Hang in there, Sisyphus buddy.

SISYPHUS: Jesus, I'm gonna need more than faith.

TANTALUS: Say…you got anything to drink?

SISYPHUS: Huh?

TANTALUS: I'm so damned parched. I really got to get something to drink.

SISYPHUS: O K. Just let me just get this rock in place here, I think I can get it to stay this time.

TANTALUS: Alright, but please do hurry.

(ORPHEUS *enters.*)

TANTALUS: Orpheus?! Dead? Oh, that sucks.

ORPHEUS: I'm still alive.

SISYPHUS: That's what they all think when they first get here.

ORPHEUS: I'm here to get Eurydice back.

TANTALUS: Your own private hell. A futile and endless search for your wife through the Underworld. That's what you've chosen and you don't even know it.

ORPHEUS: I'm still alive and I need to find Death. Have you seen her?

SISYPHUS: So if you're still alive...are the rumors true you're breaking up the band?

ORPHEUS: Look, I need to find Death. What do I have to do? It's really no picnic down here.

TANTALUS: Funny to actually find someone looking for Death instead of running away.

ORPHEUS: Can you help me?

SISYPHUS: Sure, just...let me get this...rock here settled.

ORPHEUS: I don't have time.

SISYPHUS: It'll only be another minute.

ORPHEUS: Tantalus?

TANTALUS: Sure. I just need to get a drink of water first.

ORPHEUS: Here.

(ORPHEUS *reaches in and splashes water at* TANTALUS *who again bites air but remains unquenched.*)

ORPHEUS: Never mind, I'll find Death on my own.

(*A crack of thunder. Smoke. All kinds of weird scary shit, and* DEATH *enters, trailed by her two assistants.*)

ORPHEUS: Wow.

DEATH: Death knows how to make an entrance.

TANTALUS: It's hard not to notice when Death comes into a room.

DEATH: You have something to say to me?

ORPHEUS: Sing to you actually.

DEATH: What, one of those crappy In Your Thrace songs all the kids are listening to? Spare me.

ORPHEUS: No, this one's from the soul.

DEATH: Oh, from the soul, well then, let me pull up a chair. Please. You know nothing about souls.

ORPHEUS: It's a love song. I want to bring Eurydice back.

DEATH: A love song? What is "love"? It's easy to define Death, but can you put a definition on love?

ORPHEUS: Love is not something you prove, it's something you feel.

DEATH: Oh very pretty. Yes. Thank you. But it's a little bit vague. Allow us.

(DEATH, #1, *and* #2 *put on a show. A vaudeville circus. Music. Singing [The following are the lyrics to "What is Love" music by Lewis Flinn, lyrics by Lewis Flinn and Jeremy Dobrish]*)

DEATH: Love:

#1: Lufu.

#2: Akin to luba.

#1: Lubo. To be fond of.

#2: Desire.

#1: Whence

#2: Libido.

DEATH: Lief.

#2: Like Garrett?

#1: Makes you feel like you're on

#2: fire.

DEATH: Lust.

#1: A tender

#2: feeling of affection.

DEATH: Attachment or devotion

#2: to a person.

#1: An expression of

#2: one's love or affection for.

DEATH: As in give Clytaemnestra my love!

#1: Intense

#2: affection

DEATH: for another person

#2: based on familial

#1: ties.

#2: A feeling

#1: of brotherhood

#2: good will towards others.

DEATH: Almost brings a tear to my

#2: eyes.

DEATH: How Will Rogers.

#1: A liking

#2: enthusiasm

DEATH: interest in

#2: something.

#1: A love of music.

DEATH: Oh, how appropriate.

#1: A strong,

#2: passionate,

#1: affection of

#2: one person for another.

DEATH: Here we go:

#1: Deep

#2: affection,

#1: tenderness,

#2: concern for a person with whom one has

#1: a relationship

#2: based on

DEATH: Say it

#1: sexual attraction.

#2: For who?

#1: Sexual attraction

#2: For me.

DEATH: The person who's the object of such affection.

#1 & #2: Oo-ah-chiddy-chiddy-mmm

DEATH: Intense Sexual Passion. Sexual Intercourse! That one's my favorite.

#1: A love

#2: affair.

#1: Emotional attachment,

DEATH: as held for a pet like
#1: Cerberus.
#2: Cupid.
#1: Eros
#2: The God of Love
#1: in classical mythology.
#2: Venus.
DEATH: Tennis:
#1: a score
#2: denoting zero.
DEATH: Theological:
#1: God as hero.
#1 & #2: His concern and mercy towards man.
DEATH: How touching.
#2: To feel
#1: to feel love for.
#2: Show love by embracing,
#1: or fondling,
#2: or kissing.
#1: Delight
#2: take pleasure in
DEATH: a love of books
#1: To gain
#2: to benefit
DEATH: Ooh interesting.
#1: As in a plant that loves the shade.
#2 & DEATH: Thrive on.
#1: Need.

#2 & DEATH: To feel the emotion

#1: of love.

#2: Be in love.

#1: Fall in love with.

#2: To feel love for.

#1: "For love" as a favor.

#2: For pleasure,

#1: no payment.

#2: For the love of—

#1: for the sake of.

#2: In love

#1: feel love.

#2: enamored.

#1: Make love.

#2: To woo

#1: to embrace.

#2: to kiss,

#1: *(et cetera)*,

#1 & #2: as lovers do.

DEATH: Expressions:

#1: All is fair in love and war

#2: love makes the world go round

#1: love is blind.

#2: unkind

#1 & #2: makes you funky in the mind

#1: love thy neighbor as thyself—

#2: love animals don't eat them

#1: make love

#2: not war

#1 & #2: love leaves you wanting more

#1: `tis better to have loved and lost

#2: than never loved at all

#1: no love lost

#2: no love found

#1, #2, &DEATH: Is it love that's got you down?

DEATH: Synonyms Everyone!:

#1: affection, devotion,

#2: infatuation,

SISYPHUS: fondness, passion,

TANTALUS: ejaculation

#1: beloved, heartthrob,

#2: endless compassion

SISYPHUS: worship, adore,

#1: white hot passion!

DEATH: Excellent. Well done. Bring it home:

#1 & #2: All you need is Love

DEATH: That special feelin'

#1 & #2: Love

DEATH: it's got ya reelin'

#1: love is what we're lookin' for

#2: hello love, I'm an open door

DEATH: Give me an L

#1 & #2: L

DEATH: Give me an O

#1 & #2: O

DEATH: Give me a V

#1 & #2: V

DEATH: Give me an E

#1 & #2: E

DEATH: What's that spell?

#1 & #2: LOVE

(The song ends.)

DEATH: Et cetera! And yet with all those words you mortals use, I still don't have the slightest clue what the fuck love really is.

ORPHEUS: Well I do. So don't punish me because I can feel something you can't.

DEATH: Ooh! Sassy! So sure of yourself are you? Are you sure she loves you? How?

ORPHEUS: I don't know and I don't care. I just know that she does.

DEATH: Stop wasting my time. *(She starts to exit.)*

ORPHEUS: Wait.

DEATH: Death waits for no one.

*(*ORPHEUS *goes into a cone of light, silently singing his song to* DEATH.*)*

DEATH: Well. I'm moved. Alright, I'll tell you what. Let's make a deal. You may take her back with you.

ORPHEUS: I can…?

DEATH: But these are my conditions. You will follow the path out of the Underworld and back to Earth. If she truly loves you, she will follow you out. But you must not, under any circumstance, speak to her or turn around to look at her. Once you are back to Earth, if she is still behind you, she shall be yours again.

ORPHEUS: That's it?

DEATH: That is all.

ORPHEUS: No other strings?

DEATH: My offer is as you hear it.

ORPHEUS: How do I know she'll really be behind me?

DEATH: If you have faith she is behind you, you will succeed.

ORPHEUS: And if I fail?

DEATH: Then you will lose her forever.

ORPHEUS: Alright. Deal.

(ORPHEUS *and* DEATH *shake hands.*)

DEATH: One word of advice: the promise of death is stronger than the faith of man.

ORPHEUS: I said I'll do it.

DEATH: So be it. When you begin your ascent she will follow.

(DEATH *exits with her assistants.*)

ORPHEUS: Her exits aren't as flashy as her entrances.

SISYPHUS: She was just showing off.

TANTALUS: Nice work Orpheus.

ORPHEUS: Well, I have to get going.

TANTALUS: Well, good seeing you.

SISYPHUS: We'll see you again soon I hope. I mean... well, not soon.

ORPHEUS: Good luck with...everything. *(He exits.)*

SISYPHUS: So what were we talking about?

Scene Twenty-three
ORPHEUS IN THE UNDERWORLD

(ORPHEUS' *ascent. His voice is once again amplified.*)

ORPHEUS: This deal's too good. Of course my wife loves me. I have faith. I need no definition. No proof. I have faith. My love's beyond the laws of this cruel world.

(ORPHEUS *takes a deep breath and then very quickly overcomes [undoes?] his descent. He returns to the top of his plight downward into the Underworld.*)

ORPHEUS: And so I'm here. "Abandon all hope you who enter..." Ha. I defy you. And you will deify me. For I am Orpheus, whose love was so heroic, that only he could triumph over any doubt and restitute his wife from out the Underworld. My love will now be hailed for centuries as Love, the truest love that ever was! Just one more step and I am through.

(ORPHEUS *closes his eyes. He steps through. Exquisitely sublime sounds fill the theatre. The lights of heaven open up and pour down.* ORPHEUS *stands victorious. Then a quick restore of lights, sound, and body.*)

ORPHEUS: Just one more step and I am through.

(*Long pause*)

ORPHEUS: I must know. I must know!

(ORPHEUS *turns around. He reaches out to grab* EURYDICE, *but as he does we hear the loud sound of a jail door slamming shut. He is prevented from touching her.*)

EURYDICE: (*V O*) Oh Orpheus, you cannot know. Until we meet again. I'm nought.

ORPHEUS: Eurydice. No! Eurydice, no!

(*Projection: Life After Eurydice*)

Scene Twenty-four
A STUDIO

(ANDREA *appears in a spotlight. Behind her is a slide [a slide of* ORPHEUS *onstage or something].)*

ANDREA: Hi everyone, this is Andrea Siffolopolous for N T V news reporting live from Thrace. At a press conference earlier today, a spokesman for Orpheus announced that Orpheus will be retiring from music. A candlelight vigil was held outside his house by desperately sad fans to mourn the loss of the music they so love and crave. Calls, letters, and e-mail have been streaming in from all over the world to convince Orpheus to come back. Three suicides have already been reported, presumably over the loss of Orpheus's music. *(Pause)* I say let us just be grateful for the one album we do have.

Scene Twenty-five
THE NEW HOME OF ORPHEUS AND
EURYDICE

(*One week later in* ORPHEUS's *home.* ORPHEUS *has neither eaten nor slept. He stares out in a daze as if his soul has been sucked out. He is with* ARISTAEUS, *who speaks quickly.)*

ARISTAEUS: Orpheus? You were close. You were so close. You were so close, you know? You did your best. That's all there is. I mean who doesn't have a little doubt?

ORPHEUS: I didn't have what it takes. I'm nothing.

ARISTAEUS: You have to be O K with this, O K? Look. Listen, just listen. All you have to do is listen. Now, I've heard some rumors. Now they are just rumors and I am certainly not saying that they are definitely true. But I think that you will admit that such rumors are

worthy of investigation. So I would like to...either to
confirm, or if they are not true, to deny, these rumors.
You with me big O? O K. Here it is. I hear you got
some new material. I hear you got songs so good they
can Charm Charon, Sedate Cerberus and Mystify
Minos. You got lyrics so strong they can Defy Death.
So now...and God knows I feel for your loss. We all do.
There simply is nothing more tragic. But all I'm asking
is, think of the fans. Orpheus. Big O. They want to
hear these songs. I mean, assuming of course that the
rumors are true and that these songs do in fact exist.
I mean they are dying, sorry, poor choice of words
but they are desperate, O K, to hear these songs. Now
maybe you need a little more time to recover and hey,
that is not at all a problem on my end. But you have an
opportunity here, by releasing these songs, to change
people's lives. So just let me know if it's true or not.
Give the executives a little bone. Is that so much to ask?
Help me out here huh? Are the rumors true?

ORPHEUS: They're true.

ARISTAEUS: They are? You said that, right? I did not
just make that up. O K. So, O K. Now. And by asking
you this I am not in any way pressuring you. But isn't
it possible, that after some time, I, or someone, might
hear these songs?

ORPHEUS: The songs will never be heard.

ARISTAEUS: So I'm here, I'm working the angles, and
I'm wondering, is there any way at all, to get the album
out say, a little faster than never? Because "never",
as it turns out, is actually a very long time. Because
Orpheus it is your responsibility to share your gift with
the rest of the world. Because, here's the thing: A—
number one think of the fans because we know that
they are the most important. But more importantly,
B—number two. Think of Eurydice.

(ORPHEUS *rummages around a bit looking for something.*
ARISTAEUS *stays right on him.*)

ARISTAEUS: She would want you to carry on. She would
want you to make music. And she would want you to
share your beautiful poetry with the world.

ORPHEUS: I can't without her. The music once wanted
breath, now all it wants is silence. *(He has found some
knitting.)*

ARISTAEUS: For your own good. I mean, I don't want to
scare you, but…they'll kill you. I don't exaggerate here.
For those songs? They will turn on you like rabid dogs.

ORPHEUS: A world without Eurydice is a world of
silence. *(He plunges the knitting needles into his ears. This
seems to give him some peace.)*

ARISTAEUS: Ah! Oh my…! Orpheus.

ORPHEUS: You killed her. I know you did.

ARISTAEUS: What is…? You… Please. This paranoia
has to stop. Ever since…you just have to stop this.
Orpheus. I am on your side.

ORPHEUS: I can't hear your lame babbling denials
anymore. I can see that you killed her. I can even see
why you killed her. What I cannot see is the truth. The
truth she didn't want you to tell me.

ARISTAEUS: For all the things you can see, you sure are
blind.

Scene Twenty-six
THE NEW HOME OF ORPHEUS AND EURYDICE

(Same place some time later. ORPHEUS sits with his back to the audience, impassive. He is approached by BACCHE.)

BACCHE: Orpheus? I don't know if you remember me, but I am like your biggest and most hugest fan. And... we did like sleep together one time. Well, sort of, almost. Anyway. Well, first of all—will you sleep with me again? O K. I'm sorry. Maybe that was rude. I just thought, you know like, with what happened to Eurydice and everything maybe you could use some like, female companionship or whatever. But I know I'm just like dreaming. But anyway, so like, the real reason I'm here is that I'm throwing this party. And it's like a whole bunch of Bacchantes are going to be there so it's going to be real wild and stuff and what I really need is like some killer music you know? So if you could just, like, give me a tape or whatever that would be like, totally the bomb. I mean, I wasn't going to bring this up, but you do have a responsibility to us and like to the world and stuff. I mean we could crucify you. We should. If you won't play anymore that is. Hello? Are you listening to me or are you just like totally ignoring me? Orpheus? Orpheus? Hello?

(BACCHE shakes ORPHEUS by the shoulders. His head falls off.)

BACCHE: Oh Gross!

Scene Twenty-seven
A CARD TABLE

(JASON, HERCULES, *and* ARISTAEUS *play poker.*)

HERCULES: It just ain't the same without him.

JASON: No.

ARISTAEUS: They tore his head off. How angry do you have to be to tear off a man's head? They left it on his body like a sick joke.

JASON: *(In accent)* When he died...

(ARISTAEUS *and* HERCULES *stare at him.*)

JASON: *(Without accent)* When he died the rivers shed tears and overflowed.

HERCULES: I really miss him.

JASON: It's nice having his instrument as a constellation in the sky. A nice reminder.

HERCULES: It's not the same.

JASON: I'm not saying it's the...

ARISTAEUS: And of course there's the music.

HERCULES: There's always the music.

ARISTAEUS: He's even more popular now than when he was alive. We'll put out some unreleased material, some live stuff, write a book.

JASON: He'd hate it.

ARISTAEUS: Don't you dare tell me what he'd hate.

JASON: The whole thing, all of it. It would be hell for him.

ARISTAEUS: Being adored by millions is hell?

JASON: For him, yes. His own personal hell.

ARISTAEUS: He claimed to hate it.

HERCULES: He went too far. It's his own damn fault. You can't cheat death.

JASON: He did. Why'd he have to look back? I mean he made it and then he blew it.

HERCULES: I don't know.

ARISTAEUS: It simply wasn't meant to be. The power of his love wasn't strong enough.

HERCULES: How much stronger can it get?

JASON: He wouldn't have been any happier without her.

HERCULES: And so that's how he'll be remembered. After all he did on the quest for the ghost of Phrixus and The Golden Ram's fleece, with all of his amazingly beautiful music, with all of the love he had for that woman, no, he'll be remembered as the guy who petitioned Death and blew it at the last minute.

ARISTAEUS: It's a fitting end for a man without faith.

HERCULES: He had faith, are you kidding me? That's all he ever talked about.

ARISTAEUS: He talked about having a hundred percent faith but when it came down to it, he didn't have what it takes.

HERCULES: Yeah? Well love isn't meant to transcend doubt. It's as simple as that. And you know what, that's O K by me.

JASON: He was our friend.

ARISTAEUS: That doesn't make him above reproach. He doubted everything despite what he said. He doubted us.

HERCULES: No he didn't.

ARISTAEUS: His best friends. Yes he did. And what were we if not always there for him?

HERCULES: So what if he did? You're an asshole.

ARISTAEUS: And you're a bully. And so it goes.

JASON: So love is impossible?

ARISTAEUS: It's not impossible.

HERCULES: That's ridiculous.

JASON: What does it take to make love work?

(They toast.)

ARISTAEUS: Faith.

JASON: Luck.

HERCULES: A big dick.

Scene Twenty-eight
A HILLTOP

(ORPHEUS's disembodied head)

ORPHEUS: Eurydice? Eurydice? Eurydice? Eurydice?

(We hear ORPHEUS's amplified voice as ORPHEUS continues to call out:)

ORPHEUS: *(V O)* Even in death we remain separated.

ORPHEUS: Eurydice?

ORPHEUS: *(V O)* That is my hell.

ORPHEUS: Eurydice?

ORPHEUS: *(V O)* One moment in time and the course of eternity is changed. I can no longer sing.

ORPHEUS: Eurydice?

ORPHEUS: *(V O)* I can no longer hear. All I can do is call out.

ORPHEUS: Eurydice…Eurydice…Eurydice…Eurydice… Eurydice…Eurydice…

(As ORPHEUS *continues to call out,* EURYDICE, *in her wedding dress and veil, is revealed standing very close to* ORPHEUS *but unseen by him. As* ORPHEUS *continues to call out,* EURYDICE *goes to lift her veil and reveal her face, but as she does the lights…)*

(Blackout)

END OF PLAY